Signs of Emotional Abuse

Finding The Line Between Acceptable Human Behavior and Abuse

Lana Otoya

Table Of Contents

TABLE OF CONTENTS   3

A MESSAGE TO MY READERS   5

INTRODUCTION   11

CHAPTER ONE: SCRATCHING THE SURFACE   14

CHAPTER TWO: EMOTIONAL/PSYCHOLOGICAL ABUSE   26

SECTION 2: FINDING THE LINE BETWEEN BEING HUMAN AND BEING ABUSIVE   32

CHAPTER THREE: BAD DAY OR BAD BEHAVIOR?   32

CHAPTER FOUR: AM I BEING EMOTIONALLY ABUSED?   45

CHAPTER FIVE: AM I SURE I AM BEING EMOTIONALLY ABUSED?   64

CHAPTER SIX: SO, YOU THINK THEY MEAN IT   77

SECTION 3: TALKING ABOUT EMOTIONAL ABUSE   89

CHAPTER SEVEN: TALKING IT OUT   89

SECTION 4: A ROADMAP OUT   106

CHAPTER EIGHT: IT IS TIME TO LEAVE   106

CONCLUSION   115

REFERENCES   117

A Message to My Readers

Hi friend, my name is Lana. I am a professional dating coach, author of self-care books and a blogger who founded the site millennialships.com. The name of the site stands for millennial + relationships and I created this hub for women so we can talk about the relationships between self-love and finding love. In order to find love with others, you must first *love and take care of yourself.*

This is the concept that I have based my blog, and my life around and it is my mission to spread this word to others: you are the most important person in your life. No one else comes before you.

Think about your children, your parents or your best friends. You think to yourself, surely, they come first, surely, they are more important than me. Yet if you are not happy, healthy and able to provide them with true sincere love, who will they get that from? Your children need you to be happy, healthy and thriving because they look to you as an example of how to live their lives. Your friends and other loved ones need you to be joyful and giving so that they can feel loved, supported and safe.

Now does this mean you have to be an endless pot of constant happiness and joy? No. I'm not asking you to be a robot. What I'm saying is that we often give too much of ourselves to others and forget that we cannot pour from a glass that is empty. If you give too much, you'll have nothing left to give.

If you have picked up this book it is because you have found yourself in a struggling relationship. I have found myself in this position a couple times and it is one of the most emotionally draining situations I've experienced in my entire life. Relationships are full of give and take. Sometimes your partner will have a bad day. Sometimes he or she will get angry or lash out, but when do certain behaviors cross the line from a "bad day" to abusive? When is it acceptable human behavior rather than abuse? At one point does behavior turn into abuse?

I wrote this book because the line is nearly impossible to see when you're inside an abusive relationship. I know many friends and acquaintances who would be downright offended if I told them they were in an abusive relationship, yet it doesn't make what I'm saying not true. How is it that I can see so easily that they are in an abusive relationship, and they can't see it themselves? It's because the term "love is blind" was created for a reason. This book is meant as a guide to help you determine whether you're dealing with either healthy or abusive behavior. I am here to help you draw that line so that you can find happiness and relief in your life.

Remember to take a deep look into your relationship and ask yourself: would I be ok with my daughter being in this kind of relationship? What about my best friend? Would I trade lives with the ones I love most? If your answer is no, we're already starting to get somewhere.

As you go through this book, remember that I am your friend and your guide. I am not criticizing, shaming or judging your decisions or mistakes. You are human after all, and I am simply here to take that little feeling you have in your gut and give it a bigger voice. I wish you the best in going through this book as it may not be easy, but it is sure to be eye opening and helpful. I am on your side and I want you to take your life into your own hands. You are in the driver seat my friend, I'm simply the passenger with Google maps.

GET YOUR

FREE

10 DAY SELF CARE CHALLENGE

—

*10 Days of Actionable Tasks
all in one PDF*

*VISIT:
millennialships.com/free-
self-care-challenge*

Introduction

Whenever you Google or start doing a little more research on emotional abuse, you'll always come across someone saying "physical abuse is easy to spot but emotional abuse is not so simple, it's much more difficult to see if you're being emotionally abused." I agree with what that statement is trying to get across, but I question as to whether or not emotional abuse can be "seen" because I think it can.

I know a couple where the man is emotionally abused by the woman. I can see the abuse in his behavior easily. If he says something that she doesn't agree with, he immediately changes his mind. If she asks him to get up and do something for him, he does so even if he was busy or preoccupied with something else. This man is living in fear, and fear is not part of a loving relationship. If you feel fear in your relationship, this is a glaring giant sign that your partner might be abusive.

Another way you can "see" abuse is by paying attention to how often your relationship makes you cry. People in healthy and loving relationships rarely make each other cry. Pay attention to how often you cry, and this will start giving you a great introduction to spotting emotional abuse in your own life.

And finally, you can "see" emotional abuse by looking at how often you talk negatively or complain about your partner. If you are inclined to ask your friends for "help" or "advice" on a regular basis, this is not a good sign. This may not be a sign of emotional abuse but it's definitely not a sign of a healthy loving relationship. What is stopping you from discussing these issues with your partner? If your partner can't sit down with you and have a conversation without it turning into a fight, this is not healthy behavior.

Abuse can be found in any relationship you might find yourself a part of; it could be a romantic relationship, or even a relationship with your closest friend. If you have picked this book up, there might be some signs in one of your relationships that have you worried. Maybe you are reading for a friend, and maybe you want to arm yourself with the knowledge that can help you navigate the sticky world of relationships.

Whatever your reason for picking this book up is, one

thing is certain - you will put it down having learned all you need to in order to understand the difference between a healthy relationship and one in which you are being abused. Sometimes, it can be hard to face the reality that we are in an abusive situation, and making excuses for a person becomes second nature but, what happens when you lose yourself in the abuse?

Emotional abuse is a serious issue that many people go through and do not speak up about because they do not think what they are experiencing is severe. The goal of this book is to introduce you to the different kinds of emotional abuse that you can experience in a relationship. While reading, you will discover what emotional abuse is, how to spot it in a relationship and what to do about it once you know.

If you need to talk to someone, call the National Domestic Violence Hotline at 1-800-799-SAFE (7233), or 1-800-787-3224. They can provide you with resources to help you in your situation outside of this book. If you do not want to talk to someone over the phone, there is a live chat option on their website www.thehotline.org.Read on to find out more about emotional abuse, and how you take back control of your relationship.

Chapter One: Scratching the Surface

Understanding Why It's Difficult to Pin Point Emotional Abuse

Abusive behavior can be hard to define or prove and many people think that abuse is an "opinion". I mentioned earlier that I know a couple where the man is emotionally abused by the woman. I have often heard his friends say things like "well if she makes him happy then it's ok", or "if he's ok with then I guess it's alright."

If you were saying these things about your own relationship you might say "yeah, but I don't mind it when he does that" or "but I know he doesn't mean it that way". You are saying these things as if abuse is an opinion-based thing when it really isn't. There is a line that changes things and moves behavior over into the abuse category and *you do not* get to determine where that line is.

Because emotional abuse can seem like it's based on personal opinion, it can be extremely hard to pin point. I wish I could give you a scale or a graph and say, here is when it's abusive but unfortunately, it's not that easy. The best way to start narrowing things down is by learning about the different kinds of abusive behaviors and seeing whether or not your partner's behavior falls into these categories.

Another reason why emotional abuse is so hard to pin point is that it involves creating a villain out of someone that you love. One very important thing to understand is that *emotionally abusive relationships start out healthy.*

Abusive behavior does not start right away otherwise no one would ever find themselves in a romantic relationship with abuse because they would leave instantly. If you started seeing someone and one week in, they're telling you that you can't do anything right or that they will kill themselves if you leave, you'd start to see these red flags immediately. There's no way you're sticking around with someone who acts like that.

The problem is that abuse starts to form slowly and

over a long period of time. By the time it has developed into full blown abuse, the victim is often very emotionally attached to the abuser and sometimes their lives are tied together. The couple might live together or have a child, making it a lot more difficult to leave the situation.

As a defense mechanism, your brain will then start to convince you that the abusive behavior you are dealing with "isn't that bad" or is "ok" for one reason or another. You are doing this to defend the person you love (the abuser) and you will do anything not to make that person look like the villain. Admitting that you are being abused turns your loved one into a villain and this is a very difficult thing to admit to oneself.

There are many kinds of abusive behaviors, and these fall under six larger umbrella terms that define them. You might only be familiar with one or two, but, through the course of this book, you will learn to interpret the signs of the other types of abuse too.

In order to properly diagnose abuse from inside a relationship, you must stop thinking so much about the abuser as a person. I know that sounds a little weird, but you need to remove the person you love and simply focus on the *behavior*. So when we talk about "belittling comments" you need to look at the words being said and the comments being made rather than "my boyfriend John." This act of separation is easier said than done but the goal here is to view your relationship as an outsider. You need to take an objective look at your relationship and stop viewing it from rose colored glasses.

Let's try to do that by taking a look at the different types of abuse. This is the first way you can exercise viewing your relationship through an objective lens. Think about the behaviors that are common in your relationship rather than the person behind those actions.

There is no set formula for how abuse happens and why, but there are a list of behaviors and attitudes to watch out for and examine in your relationship to ensure your safety.

To break down and understand what an abusive situation is or looks like, you need to understand what abuse is, and how to change the situation.

This is not another one of those books that just tells you about abuse. I seek to illustrate what abuse types look like and how to accurately depict if you are in an abusive situation. I created this interactive model that will help you see your situation more objectively.

6 Types of Abuse

We will briefly cover the six main types of abuse. The various types of abuse range from physical abuse, emotional abuse, verbal abuse, sexual abuse, financial abuse, neglect, and there are still more. Abuse really varies in the forms that it appears in.

When you're reading through these different kinds of abuse, you can use this as a way to test yourself. For example, you can read through a type of abuse, its definition, and ask yourself whether that kind of abuse is present in your relationship. If you say "no, that's not in my relationship" that's excellent, we can move onto the next one. If you find yourself hesitating or saying "that *may* be present in my relationship" just pencil that one and we can look into it deeper as we go through this book.

The key here is to use these definitions as a guide to

help you step outside of your relationship and look inward with un-biased opinions as much as possible.

Physical Abuse

Physical abuse, the most obvious one occurs when one person in a relationship threatens physical bodily harm or uses external force against another in order to intimidate or keep control of them. It is important to remember that physical abuse does not have to result in bruises or cuts to be considered abuse. The threat alone of physically harming another person can be classified as physical abuse.

This type of abuse can appear in many different forms. If you are concerned that either you or someone you know might be in a relationship dominated by physical abuse, have a look at the signs that indicate abuse is occurring. Physical abuse can happen when a person bites, slaps, chokes, kicks, punches or pulls your hair.

Forbidding a person from eating food or being allowed to sleep is another direct example of physical abuse. While they are not laying a finger on you, they are using physical intimidation to get a result that does not benefit you. Physical abuse also includes being hurt with any sort of weapon, being prevented from calling the police or getting help, and driving recklessly when in the same vehicle.

These are just a few examples of ways in which physical abuse can manifest itself. Keep in mind; there are always other signs in which physical abuse demonstrates itself.

Verbal Abuse

Verbal abuse is often overlooked as a form of abuse, but it can have lasting effects on a person. Verbal abuse can happen when body language and words are used to criticize or put down another person viciously.

The goal of a person perpetrating verbal abuse against another is to lower their self-esteem and lead them to believe that they are not worthy of respect or love. It can also manifest itself as a derogatory way of telling someone they have no talent or abilities to accomplish their goals.

The reason verbal abuse is so damaging is because it is often not recognized as abuse and, when left unchecked for periods of times, it not only devalues the person being abused, but it can also cause them to miss opportunities in life they otherwise might have taken.

Emotional Abuse

Emotional abuse is an umbrella term to describe a situation where an abuser's behavior causes emotional stress or harm on the victim. Emotional stress can be depression, anxiety, PTSD or any other psychological or mental trauma. We will be discussing all aspects of emotional abuse in much more detail throughout this book.

Sexual Abuse

Any sexual contact that is unwanted is sexual abuse. It can occur in any relationship in a variety of ways and is extremely damaging to a person. Sexual abuse shows itself when an abuser forces you to dress or act in a sexual way, manipulates or forces you into doing or performing sexual acts, holds you down during sex, and even intentionally passing a known sexual disease to you.

These are only a few of the many ways in which sexual abuse occurs. Sexual abuse can also include the coercion or manipulation into having sex, for example, if an abuser makes you feel like you owe them something, or if they give you drugs to "get you ready" for sexual acts.

Sexual abuse that occurs within a long-term relationship is often hard to prove. Abusers of children and adults alike often threaten their victims with bodily harm if they tell anyone that they are being abused, and their cycle of abuse continues.

Financial Abuse

Financial abuse occurs when one person holds money or finances over another person. This could mean not giving them access to their own bank account by keeping their debit card or credit card. It could also mean stealing or using money without permission or simply not allowing the victim to get a job and make their own money. Abusers will often use finances as a way to make the victim dependent or reliant on them. If an abuser is the breadwinner and brings home all the household income, they can use this as a way to keep a victim trapped and locked into the relationship.

Neglect

Neglect is the final category of abuse and it happens to people who are unable to take care of themselves. Children, the elderly and people with mental or physical disabilities are the most common victims of neglect. If someone cannot meet their basic human needs on their own, they will need the help of another person. If the other person fails to provide these basic human needs, they are neglecting the victim. A simple example is with a toddler. A toddler is unable to provide food and shelter for itself and if a capable adult does not provide these things to the toddler, that would be considered neglect.

Abuse Takes Many Forms

There are still many other abuse types not highlighted that can fall under the same category or even in their own niche, but recognizing the signs that abuse can manifest itself in can help you detect the signals early on and find an escape route.

A few takeaways from this chapter include:

- It's extremely difficult to diagnose emotional abuse from insde a relationship. In order to do so, you'll need to try your best to see your relationship from an outsider's perspective.

- There are 6 main types of abuse. Going through each one and asking yourself if that type of abuse is present in your relationship is a good way to start seeing things objectively.

- It is easier to define abuse when you know what abusive behavior looks like.

I gave a brief overview of some other common abusive types. The focus of this book, however, is going to be on abuse that is not often discussed but is extremely damaging to the psyche. This abuse contains elements of verbal abuse, and they are often combined under the same blanket term. In the next chapter, I will define and highlight the ways in which emotional abuse occurs. When a person understands what emotional abusive behavior is, they are better prepared to handle it when they experience it, and it is often easier for them to find their way out of the situation.

Chapter Two: Emotional/Psychological Abuse

Breaking Down Emotional Abuse

Emotional abusers use a person's feelings in order to mess with their head and get them to comply with their wishes. Similar to verbal abuse, emotional abuse is often not recognized in its early stages, so the long-term ramifications for victims are often severe. If victims are able to pick up on the early signs of emotional abuse occurring, they are more likely to get help or to get out of the situation.

While it is critical to identify when emotional abuse is happening to you, there are some instances that are not classified as abuse. Since it is so hard to identify, knowing what scenarios do not fall under emotional abuse can also help separate abusive behaviors from non-abusive behaviors.

Some instances that are not a situation of emotional abuse are:

- When a partner breaks up with you.

- A simple disagreement or argument with a partner.

- If someone is hurt by your actions.

- When someone occasionally yells to express their emotions.

These situations above are not considered to be emotionally abusive. When the behavior occurs in an excessive manner that begins to affect your self-perception, then it might be time to re-evaluate the relationship and its effect on you.

It is important to fully understand what is being said here. The line of abuse can be drawn somewhere in between a behavior happening *once* and *often*. Here are some examples:

- If a partner raises his voice and gets angry once every four months, this is not abusive. If he or she raises their voice and gets angry every day, this *is* abusive.

- If a partner just suffered a serious life event, let's say they lost their job and they come home and express their anger physically on an inanimate object, this is not abuse. If a partner is constantly breaking or throwing things, this is abusive.

As you can see, certain behaviors can be classified as healthy or abusive depending on how often they occur. As we move forward through the information and exercises in this book, it'll be a lot easier to see how often is "too often" and when behavior has crossed the line. For now, just understand that the *frequency* at which a behavior occurs has a big impact on whether or not it is normal or abusive.

It Is an Umbrella Term

Emotional abuse is regarded as *any* abusive behaviors that do not involve physical violence. This can include humiliation, manipulation, intimidation, and verbal assaults, whose aims are to eradicate a person's sense of self-worth, dignity, and identity. The long-term ramifications from emotional abuse are suicidal thoughts or behaviors, post-traumatic stress disorder (PTSD), depression and anxiety.

Since emotional abuse is such a broad term, it can house a lot of abusive behaviors that damage and affect a victim's mental state.

Interestingly, emotional abuse and physical abuse cycles follow the same patterns. Once the victim realizes the behaviors going on, the abuser tends to adjust their behaviors temporary or further guilt the victim into believing they were in error.

Some signs of emotionally abusive behavior can include:

- Constantly being told you cannot do anything right.

- Extreme jealousy at any time spent away from partner.

- Discourages you from seeing friends or family; isolates you.

- Controls what you do, where you go and whom

you see.

- Blaming you for the abuse you make them do to you.

- Gaslighting (when your partner uses techniques to make you question everything you know. Slowly drives you crazy.)

There are so many more ways in which emotional abuse manifests itself, and these are only a few key behaviors that you can look for to identify emotional abuse.

Remember, it does not always seem apparent to you when you or someone you know is being emotionally abusive. We often make excuses for our loved ones in these situations, but the longer we remain in an abusive situation, the worse your mental health becomes.

Key Points

Keep in mind that emotional abuse can manifest itself in a relationship in different ways. Here is a quick run through of those ways:

- Emotional abuse can have long-term mental side effects on a victim.

- These side effects can include depression and be as severe as having PTSD (post-traumatic stress disorder).

- Victims often make excuses for their abuser's behaviors.

- If you are being isolated from family and friends, this is a big sign that you are being emotionally abused.

- Emotional abuse is interchangeable with other terms like psychological abuse and mental abuse.

Over the next few sections and chapters, I will go more in depth about what to do about emotional abuse, how to find out if your relationship is emotionally abusive, and a roadmap out of your abusive situation.

Remember! Emotional abuse can occur in more than just a romantic relationship. A parent-child relationship or even just a friendship can have signs of emotional abuse as well.

Section 2: Finding the Line Between Being Human and Being Abusive

Chapter Three: Bad Day or Bad Behavior?

Being Human or Being Abusive

Okay, so we have all been there. You have had a bad day, and you take it out on someone you should not. Maybe you yell a little too loud, or maybe you say something you later wish you had not. Does this mean you are an emotional abuser?

There is a line between being human and being abusive. People have bad days, and people have disagreements. This does not necessarily mean they are abusive, so how do you tell then if your partner is just having a bad day,

—

or if they are emotionally abusing you?

Keep track of behavior patterns. Ask yourself after interactions with your partner; "How did that make me feel?" When a set of behaviors become a consistent pattern, it goes from a bad day to abusive. A disagreement with your partner does not necessarily constitute emotional abuse, and if your feelings get hurt from something they said, it might just be a bad moment for them.

If your partner has a disagreement with you or yells at you after a bad day, they might regret it. If they are willing to be open and communicate about it, it makes it easier for you to find that line between abuse and a bad moment. Listen to what your partner says when they are discussing the argument. A key element of emotional abuse is that an abuser will try to make you feel bad or guilty for the argument. They will tell you it was your fault.

Take that as a red flag. A partner who has a bad day should be able to communicate when they have done something wrong without making you feel responsible for it. A sign of emotional abuse to look for is when they are blaming you for the abuse.

Let me stop for a moment and clarify. You are not to blame for the abuse. Yes, they might say this and make you feel like you are, but that is what an emotional abuser does, and they are good at what they do. So, if you find yourself in a situation where you are being blamed for the abusive behavior done to you, and you find yourself believing that you were the one at fault, take a step back. Analyze the situation and your emotions. When you do this, you might find you notice other key behaviors of theirs that indicate you are the victim of an emotional abuser.

Overreacting after a bad day is a normal, healthy behavior. It happens to the best of us. Normal and healthy behavior also includes looking back on one's actions and apologizing if they have done something to hurt someone.

Intent is a very important thing to pay attention to when analyzing abusive behavior. Let's look at an example.

Let's say your partner comes home from a very bad day, they were fired at work and will not be able to pay this month's rent. This is a very serious situation and when they get home from work, they can't help but get angry and punch the wall. When they do this, a favorite vase of yours gets knocked off the shelf and breaks. You are now angry and upset by your partner's behavior are sad that a valuable of yours has been broken.

The behavior in itself so far is *not* emotionally abusive. In order to analyze if the behavior is healthy or turns into emotional abuse, we must look at *intent*. When your partner has calmed down, you let them know that the way they acted resulted in a broken item of yours that you loved very much, and you're upset about it. Let's analyze two possible reactions.

Healthy reaction: "I didn't mean to break your favorite vase, I was just so upset about what happened at work and I cannot even fathom what I'm going to do with my life now."

Abusive reaction: "I can't believe you care more about that stupid vase than you do about my career. Don't you understand that I got fired? I'm only going to work so that we can afford that house that you want."

Do you see the difference in those two reactions? One of them understands how you feel about the vase and makes it clear that the intention was never to hurt you. The other makes you feel guilty for bringing up your feelings and makes it seem like you are feeling upset because of your own doing.

I feel that the abusive line in the above example is quite easy to spot. Let's make the lines of abuse a little less obvious but analyzing the following reactions.

Healthy reaction: "Do you care more about that vase than my career? I'm really upset right now and need some support."

Abusive reaction: "You're always overreacting. I can't believe you care more about that vase than my career."

Now things are getting tricky! Let's analyze.

The first reaction is healthy because asking if you care more about the vase than your career is definitely rude, but it's a fair point to bring up. At this time your partner is not in a mood to deal with the broken vase and so they want to turn the focus back on their problem. The subject is then changed to your partner telling you that they are upset and asking for support. Y partner is doing a great job at reminding you that right now they are not in a happy state of mind and need you to support them in this time of need. It is implied that the vase situation can be dealt with later and although this reaction is not perfect, it is perfectly acceptable considering the kind of emotional stress the person is under at this time.

The second reaction is abusive because saying "you're always overreacting" is a total dismissal of your feelings and implies that you always act in a way that this person does not approve of. This basically means "your feelings don't matter". This is not healthy behavior because both partners' feelings should always matter enough to be brought up for discussion. The second line "I can't believe you care more about that vase than my career" is also crossing the abusive line because it is putting words into your mouth. You never said you cared *more* about the vase, you simply said that you cared about it. A partner that paints you out to be the bad guy is looking for a fight and not looking to work together.

The second reaction also does not ask for your help or support. An abusive partner often has trouble communicating their needs in a healthy way. I'm sure the abusive partner would appreciate some support, but they are not bringing it up because they don't know how to communicate effectively. 2:50 PMsimply tell you that your feelings don't matter and then put words into your mouth to make you look like the bad guy.

You might now be thinking "wow this emotional abuse thing can get complicated" and you are correct. Emotional abuse is *very* nuanced. A sentence with the same meaning can be either abusive or healthy depending on the way it is phrased. Let's look at another example.

Let's pretend that you *do* look fat in a dress and you ask your partner if the dress makes you look fat. Let's look at two responses:

Healthy response: I think you look beautiful no matter what you wear. If you want to wear that dress that's cool with me but personally, I love the blue one that you wore to the other party we went to.

Unhealthy response: Yes, that dress makes you look really fat. You have to stop eating all those snacks after dinner.

I hope the above example can help you see that phrasing does matter and emotionally abusive partners nearly always choose the wrong way to phrase things. They phrase things in a way that are unhelpful and make you *feel bad.*

Gaslighting

I want to take a moment and draw attention to a very common tactic that emotional abusers use: Gaslighting. Maybe you've heard the term used before but are not sure what it means. It is commonly used by emotional abusers to skew your own perception of reality.

Gaslighting is the practice of psychologically manipulating a person until they begin to question and doubt their own sanity. Since abuse is about control and power in a relationship, gaslighting is an extremely effective method of accomplishing this as it makes a victim question their sanity, their own feelings, and their gut instincts. The reason gaslighting is such a serious issue is because once an abuser gets the victim to a point where they question themselves so intensely, a victim is less likely to leave the abuser or the abusive situation.

There are a few techniques involved when an abuser uses gaslighting that are important to look out for.

Withholding is one of those techniques. Withholding is where an abuser can pretend not to understand what a victim is saying, or even refuse to listen to them. They will indicate that the victim is trying to confuse them, or not making sense.

When an abuser questions a victim's memory of events, despite the fact that the victim remembers things correctly, they are using a technique called countering. This makes a victim question their memory and, in turn, their level of sanity.

Blocking and diverting are other key ways abusers use gaslighting on a victim. The abuser will either change the subject, or question the victim's thoughts, to cause internal conflict within the victim.

Ever heard someone tell you that you are too sensitive, or that you get angry or emotional for no reason? When a partner is using the technique called trivializing, they make the victim's needs seem unimportant or inconsequential.

The last behavior to look for to know if you are being

gaslighted is the forgetting and denial technique. Here, an abuser will pretend to forget events or conversations that have transpired and deny things that they may have said or promised to the victim.

All these techniques are used when an abuser is trying to gaslight a victim. This is why it is important to analyze how you are feeling after interactions with your partner.

Gaslighting does not happen overnight. It occurs slowly over time in a relationship. An incident or two may seem harmless to the victim, but, over time, they will lose their sense of self, become anxious and depressed, and even feel isolated. Once the victim enters into these feelings, they begin to rely on their abusive partner more. This makes it a harder situation to escape.

If you are wanting to analyze your feelings to see if you are being gaslighted, here are some common signs victims of gaslighting experience:

- You are always second-guessing yourself.

- You do not think you are good enough to be with your partner.

- It seems like you cannot do anything right.

- You may feel confused, and even crazy.

- You are always the one to apologize to your partner.

- You remember your former self as a different person.

- You excuse your partner's behaviors not only to yourself but your friends and family.

- You feel/know something is wrong, but you cannot express it.

- You have trouble making simple choices.

- You hide information to avoid put-downs or feelings of confusion brought on by your partner.

- You feel anxiety when you're around your partner.

The above signs are a few of the most common feelings victims of gaslighting have reported to experience. If, while reading this you feel like you can identify with the feelings, take a moment to step back and evaluate the status of your relationship. If you need help, go and speak to someone outside of your partner that you can trust for advice. If you are unsure about whom you can or cannot trust, reach out for help at the National Domestic Violence Hotline by calling, or even live chatting with them if you do not want to call.

Key Points

A few important takeaways from this chapter are:

- Not all moments of anger or disagreement are abuse.

- There is a line between being human and being abusive.

- Constantly being blamed for arguments is an indicator you are being emotionally abused.

- Gaslighting is the main technique used by abusers.

- Gaslighting can leave a victim to lose a sense of themselves and their sanity.

- If you think you are being emotionally abused,

reach out to the National Domestic Violence Hotline at 1-800-799-SAFE (7233), or 1-800-787-3224.

Now that you have a better idea of the line between being human and being abusive, we will delve into some case studies, exercises and worksheets that might help you better determine whether you are in an abusive situation and what to do about it.

Chapter Four: Am I Being Emotionally Abused?

Case Studies Help

Even with the outlines and all the information given, sometimes it is still hard to depict whether we are being emotionally abused or not. If we are, it can be easy to make excuses for our own situations because the lines are blurred but, what happens when someone else is experiencing your same situation?

Case studies are an in-depth analysis of a situation, and they can help you see what an emotionally abusive situation looks like when someone else is experiencing it. If you identify with the situation and you feel outraged, scared or sadness for the people mentioned in the case study, you might want to analyze your own relationship to see if you might be excusing the same behaviors.

Diedre's Predicament

All names have been changed in the case study to protect anonymity

Diedre says that if her abuser had punched her in the face the first time they had gone out, then she would never have gone back, but the truth of what he did was so much worse. They got married after a 9-month whirlwind romance. She was in an emotionally vulnerable place, and he made her feel secure.

At first, his jealousy was endearing to Diedre. She would think it was cute that he cared that much about her. Slowly, his behavior went from subtle comments about her shoes or a skirt to telling her that people were going to be staring at her in her skimpy outfits, and, eventually just telling her she was dressed like a prostitute.

They had a daughter together that he did not parent very much. He made his wife quit her job so that she could take care of the home. When Diedre went to fetch her daughter from school, she was timed. He would call the home to ensure that she got back in an appropriate amount of time from picking their daughter up.

Diedre stayed at home, stopped seeing her friends and family and took care of him. He would come home to freshly ironed shirts and a clean house. Diedre remarks on how he always wanted the shirt that was dirty though. It did not matter how many shirts she ironed, it was always the wrong shirt.

Things really started to throw Diedre off when he would not let her go to the doctor for check-ups. Diedre's abuser told her that all she wanted was to get naked in front of a doctor. In an emergency, Diedre wound up at the doctors and found out her ovaries had to be removed. His response to her was that she had done it to spite him.

Diedre was stuck in the relationship for seven years, and she believes that if she had stayed in longer, the relationship would have killed her. He threatened to kill her in the end.

Diedre says even after three years she still goes to therapy. She believed she was worthless and her identity was gone and vanished. She remarks that she was a happy person before him; an outgoing person.

The Point in Diedre's Story

Diedre's story highlights several techniques of emotional abuse. Her abuser uses guilt to make her feel as if everything is her fault. In the previous chapters, I have highlighted the emotions that are felt by victims of emotional abuse, and Diedre depicts those in her emotional story as well.

Diedre was able to get herself help when she saw the effect the abuse was having on her own child, and it was becoming harder to deny his effect on her child. She was disorientated about what her abuser was doing to her.

He used gaslighting techniques to confuse Diedre and make her believe that there was nothing she could do right. Diedre ended up relying on her abuser for support, without realizing he was causing her to feel the way she was.

If you identify with any part of Diedre's story or emotions, keep reading. There is still lots more to cover and explore about being in an emotionally abusive situation.

—

While this particular case study does depict the abuser as male, men are not the only perpetrators of emotional abuse, and there are many cases as well where women have been emotionally abusive to men. Whether it is a male or female perpetrating the abuse, the results are the same for the victim. Getting out of an abusive situation as soon as possible is the best thing for your mental health.

Emotional Abuse Quiz

Below, there will be a brief quiz. It is easy to continue to make excuses for our partners; it becomes a little harder when the answers are staring us right back in the face. Throughout this book, we will do a few exercises that can help you navigate whether you are being emotionally abused or not. This quiz can be taken with a romantic partner in mind, or you can assess a non-romantic relationship you might have doubts about.

The quiz only works if you are one 100% honest with yourself. This quiz was created by Nteract Support.

Do you:

- Feel afraid of your partner most of the time?

  o Yes

  o No

  o At times

- Avoid certain topics out of fear of angering them?

  o Yes

  o No

  o At times

- Feel like you cannot do anything right for them?

  o Yes

  o No

  o At times

- Believe that you deserve to be mistreated or hurt?

  o Yes

- o No

- o At times

- Wonder if you are crazy?

  - o Yes

  - o No

  - o At times

- Feel emotionally numb or helpless?

  - o Yes

  - o No

  - o At times

Do they:

- Humiliate or yell at you?

  - o Yes

  - o No

  - o At times

- Criticize and put you down?

- Yes

- No

- At times

- Make you embarrassed to see family and friends?

  - Yes

  - No

  - At times

- Put down/ignore your accomplishments?

  - Yes

  - No

  - At times

- Blame you for their abusive behavior?

  - Yes

  - No

  - At times

- See you as their property?

- Yes

- No

- At times

• Have an unpredictable temper?

- Yes

- No

- At times

• Threaten to hurt or kill you?

- Yes

- No

- At times

• Threaten to take your children away?

- Yes

- No

- At times

• Threaten to commit suicide if you leave?

- Yes

- No

- At times

- Force you to have sex when you do not want to?

  - Yes

  - No

  - At times

- Act jealous and possessive to limit who you see?

  - Yes

  - No

  - At times

- Control where you go or what you do?

  - Yes

  - No

  - At times

- Isolate you from friends and family?

- Yes

- No

- At times

- Limit your access to money and transport?

  - Yes

  - No

  - At times

- Constantly check up on you?

  - Yes

  - No

  - At times

Fill in the circle if you feel like your partner is exhibiting this behavior towards you and calculate how many questions you said yes to.

The more questions that you answered yes to, the more likely you are to be in an abusive situation. If you answered yes to most of the questions, the odds are you already know you are being emotionally abused but are unsure about how to get out of it. That is okay; this is why you are reading this book. I will help you find a way to plan your way out from the situation safely.

Self-Worth is Another Indicator

Even after taking the previous quiz, you might still have some doubts. Emotional abuse is a very serious problem that often goes undetected for a long period of time. There are direct correlations between emotional abuse and a person's level of self-worth, anxiety, and depression.

Below, take the test to see where your self-worth lies. This test was modified from UWire for College Student.

1. I tend to feel pretty good about myself as a person.

    o   Strongly Disagree – 1

    o   Disagree Somewhat – 2

    o   Neutral – 3

    o   Agree Somewhat – 4

o Strongly Agree – 5

2. Most people I know are more intelligent and knowledgeable than I am.

   o Strongly Disagree – 1

   o Disagree Somewhat – 2

   o Neutral – 3

   o Agree Somewhat – 4

   o Strongly Agree – 5

3. Most people I know look more attractive than I look.

   o Strongly Disagree – 1

   o Disagree Somewhat – 2

   o Neutral – 3

   o Agree Somewhat – 4

   o Strongly Agree – 5

4. Most people are more interesting to talk to than I am.

   o Strongly Disagree – 1

- Disagree Somewhat – 2

- Neutral – 3

- Agree Somewhat – 4

- Strongly Agree – 5

5. I am often surprised to find out that other people view me in a more positive light than I see myself.

   - Strongly Disagree – 1

   - Disagree Somewhat – 2

   - Neutral – 3

   - Agree Somewhat – 4

   - Strongly Agree – 5

6. I feel like I am a pretty good partner in a relationship.

   - Strongly Disagree – 1

   - Disagree Somewhat – 2

   - Neutral – 3

   - Agree Somewhat – 4

o   Strongly Agree – 5

7. It makes me feel good about myself when I am able to complete a task that is difficult.

    o   Strongly Disagree – 1

    o   Disagree Somewhat – 2

    o   Neutral – 3

    o   Agree Somewhat – 4

    o   Strongly Agree – 5

8. To a large extent, how I feel about myself is determined by how others think of me.

    o   Strongly Disagree – 1

    o   Disagree Somewhat – 2

    o   Neutral – 3

    o   Agree Somewhat – 4

    o   Strongly Agree – 5

9. I often think negative thoughts about myself.

    o   Strongly Disagree – 1

o   Disagree Somewhat – 2

o   Neutral – 3

o   Agree Somewhat – 4

o   Strongly Agree – 5

10. I often have a hard time understanding why someone would be interested in me in a way that is romantic or sexual.

o   Strongly Disagree – 1

o   Disagree Somewhat – 2

o   Neutral – 3

o   Agree Somewhat – 4

o   Strongly Agree – 5

Now that the test is done, add together the total your answers scored. For example, the answers to questions 1 through 10 each have a number ranging from one to five. Add up your answer from each question to find out where you fall on the scale of self-worth.

If you scored between:

10-25: you seem to have a low sense of self-worth. Poor self-worth can get in the way of you accomplishing your goals and dreams. It can also make it more challenging to lead a healthy romantic relationship. This can indicate that your ideas about yourself are wrong.

26-40: You have a moderate sense of self-worth. You have some negative feelings about yourself that could be improved. Keep in mind that you do not always have to be so harsh on yourself. Think about why you think about yourself in a negative light at times.

41-50: Congrats! Your feelings of self-worth are spot on. Having a good self-worth can positively impact your romantic relationships and your ability to conquer your aspirations.

If you scored low on this test, you might want to evaluate why these feelings of low self-worth plague you. It could be because of the emotional abuse that you have received from your partner. Be honest with yourself when taking these tests.

If you scored low on this test but the previous quiz you answered that you were not emotionally abused, go up and take it one more time. Open up and be honest about how your partner makes you feel.

Key Points

Taking the quiz might have taken a lot out of you. It can be hard to face the reality that someone we think we love has been manipulating us, so I will quickly recap this chapter to keep these ideas fresh in your mind.

- Diedre's case study demonstrates how deeply emotional abuse can affect a person.

- Her case highlights the ways in which emotional abuse is perpetrated in everyday life.

- The quiz can help you identify whether your relationship is emotionally abusive.

- Emotional abuse can occur in any relationship, and it does not have to be romantically inclined.

I hope this chapter has helped you understand more about the ways in which emotional abuse crops up in our lives, and what this particular monster can look like. The next few chapters are going to have us working out some more about what emotionally abusive situations look like.

Chapter Five: Am I Sure I Am Being Emotionally Abused?

Relax, Breathe In, Breathe Out

Relationships are riddled with insecurities. There are so many factors in a relationship that can cause a person to doubt themselves. The one thing you do not want to do is accuse a partner of being emotionally abusive if you are not sure.

That is the purpose of this book, to help you navigate this sticky situation and point you in the right direction for help and resources.

Right now, you might be freaking out inside because the quiz revealed that your partnership might be emotionally abusive. Relax. I will take you through the steps and information you need to know to prepare yourself. It will not be easy, but hey! You have made it this far, and you've got a few more steps in you.

Let us take some time and go over some common misconceptions when it comes to abusive situations.

Many people believe that abuse does not happen to those in high school or college or the generally educated population. This is a false notion. Abuse can happen in any relationship regardless of gender, race, age or educational level.

Also, it can be common to believe that once a person leaves an abusive situation, that the abuse ends. This is usually the time when a victim is most at risk. Experts recommend safety planning for the victim as the abuser can be volatile during a separation.

Sometimes, friends have the best intentions but conduct them in the worst of ways. Some people believe that the best way to get a loved one to leave an abusive situation is to cut their ties with them. This is one of the worst things you can do to help a friend in an abusive situation. Because an abuser's main goal is to have their victim rely on only them, you are further isolating a friend if you cut ties with them. A victim needs support from friends and family in order to find their way out.

If you are a friend and you are reading this book to find out how to help someone out, keep reading.

Understanding their situation will give you more insight into how to help them. They might not be willing to listen to what you have to say about their relationship, but if you are armed and ready with the knowledge needed to help, you can provide more support when they need it most.

If you are the one being abused, you might be tempted to stop reaching out to your friends. You might think that they're tired of hearing about it or that they've lost interest. If you communicate with them that you're going through a tough time, good friends will understand. If you see them getting uncomfortable with how much you talk about your relationship, it's good to still keep them close. Talk to them about other aspects of your life or goals that you want to accomplish. It is in your best interest to keep a close relationship with your friends so that you do not end up isolated from everyone but your abuser.

Okay, but What if I am the Abuser?

So, maybe you took the quiz above, and you did not

identify with any of the situations. Maybe there is a nagging thought at the back of your head that you portray some of these traits towards your partner. Are you abusive?

Remember that physical abuse does not always occur in situations where there is emotional abuse. Often, there are times when the perpetrators are unaware that they are being emotionally abusive towards their partners.

They may be aware of their feelings of insecurity and jealousy about their partner, but not know how to process it. The abuser might believe that they know what is best for their partner and so, in turn, tries to control what they eat, to where they go, and how they dress. While some abusers know exactly what they are doing, it does occur that the emotional abuse displayed stems from the abuser's own feelings of inadequacy or lack of control.

If the question is still nagging at you, there is a short quiz you can take to find out if you are guilty of showing abusive behavior towards your partner. The quiz was generated by Nteract Support.

Do you:

- Make them afraid in order to control their behavior?

    o Yes

    o No

    o At times

- Stop them from talking about things that upset you?

    o Yes

    o No

    o At times

- Make them check everything with you first because they cannot be trusted?

    o Yes

    o No

    o At times

- Verbally hurt them to keep control?

    o Yes

- o No

- o At times

- Make them think they are crazy when they defy you?

  - o Yes

  - o No

  - o At times

- Play games and deny what you have said or act as if you were joking if they get upset about something you say?

  - o Yes

  - o No

  - o At times

- Believe that you are the one with the right to make up all the rules?

  - o Yes

  - o No

  - o At times

- Yell at, or humiliate them if they annoy you?

    o Yes

    o No

    o At times

- Criticize them to keep them in place?

    o Yes

    o No

    o At times

- Isolate them from spending time with other people?

    o Yes

    o No

    o At times

- Ignore or put down their accomplishments?

    o Yes

    o No

    o At times

- Tell them it is their fault if you get angry or abuse them?

  o Yes

  o No

  o At times

- Believe that they belong to you and should do as you say?

  o Yes

  o No

  o At times

- Have a bad and unpredictable temper?

  o Yes

  o No

  o At times

- Threaten to hurt them if they push you too far?

  o Yes

  o No

o At times

- Threaten to take their children away if they try to leave you?

  o Yes

  o No

  o At times

- Threaten to commit suicide if they leave?

  o Yes

  o No

  o At times

- Have sex with them even if they do not want to?

  o Yes

  o No

  o At times

- Feel jealous and possessive over them?

  o Yes

  o No

o At times

- Control what they do and where they go?

  o Yes

  o No

  o At times

- Keep them from seeing friends and family?

  o Yes

  o No

  o At times

- Make them give you receipts and change back when you give them money?

  o Yes

  o No

  o At times

- Track them electronically, or check up on them constantly?

  o Yes

- o No

- o At times

- Read their mail, texts or emails without their knowledge?

  - o Yes

  - o No

  - o At times

The more answers you have answered yes to, the higher the likelihood that you are being emotionally abusive. All these questions signal behaviors that indicate emotional abuse is taking place.

If you answered yes to most of the above questions, then you might have been told you are abusive, or aware that you are. There are resources to assist you as well if you want to change your ways and learn how to be in a healthy relationship. Do not resist counseling. Counseling can be a wonderful benefit to help someone out who is an emotional abuser and help them resolve the feelings that cause them to manipulate others.

What do you do if you are in a relationship but still want to stay together? It is vital that both the abuser and the victim go through counseling and therapy separately. As emotional abuse has long-term ramifications on a victim, if you are aware of your behaviors, take immediate action for both you and your partner. Allow your partner to complete therapy and make their own decisions. If you both decide to move forward, the next step will be couples' therapy together.

Key Points

Wow! What a lot of information. Here are a few highlights:

- If you are being abused, there is always help. There is a way out.

- If you are the abuser, there is help too! Be proactive and seek out help for yourself.

- Abuse can happen to anyone; it does not happen only within a certain group.

- The most dangerous time for a victim is when they get ready to leave their abuser.

Change is possible, both if you are the victim or the abuser. As a victim, you can find your way out and back to yourself again. As an abuser, you can find help for yourself and locate where your need to control stems from. Some people stay together despite a situation that involves abuse; some people stay apart.

The important thing to know is that if you are being abused, you need to get out and get some help. You cannot save your partner, and it is not your job to secure their emotional security because you need to work on your own. You lose yourself when you are in an emotionally abusive relationship, and the first person you need to help is yourself.

Chapter Six: So, You Think They Mean It

Why You Cannot Help Them

"Alyssa" read a magazine article that finally helped her understand why her husband was so controlling. He took charge of everything, from what they ate, to what she did, and even how she dressed.

At first, Alyssa thought it was endearing that he put so much thought into her clothes and how she presented itself. She even liked that he ordered food for her when they went out, and she never minded cooking his favorite meals for him at home; she wanted him to be happy.

Alyssa did not like it when he suggested she quit her job, but, after he came home and was yelling at how he never has the clothes he wants to wear clean; she understood his point of view.

Maybe it had seemed odd before to Alyssa that she never saw her family anymore and that her friends had stopped coming around a while ago, but it never clicked until she saw that article about emotional abuse. Now she knew how to help her husband! She just had to get him to talk to her.

The problem with Alyssa's situation above is that often victims of emotional abuse do not understand the gravity of their situation. Alyssa cannot help her husband as long as she remains in an emotionally abusive environment.

A person that is an emotional abuser will not be open to your discussion that they have been emotionally abusing you. More often than not, they will turn the situation around and make you feel guilty for doubting them in the first place. You will find yourself trapped in the cycle of emotional abuse all over again as you internalize your conflict over their abuse.

Sometimes, the victim can even feel like they deserve the abuse. Let me be clear here, under no circumstances does a victim deserve the abuse they are receiving.

The absolute worst thing you can say to an emotional abuser is that you feel emotionally abused. As a victim of emotional abuse, your primary concern should not be how to talk the problem out with your partner, but how to protect yourself. You need to be aware of the dangers of repeating the cycle of emotional abuse and finding yourself help to deal with the psychological damage the abuse has already done to you.

Remember that a victim of emotional abuse can have severe depression, anxiety and even feel as if they are losing their sanity, so it is important you get yourself to a trusted place for help and therapy. There is no easy path or way to heal from emotional abuse.

Emotional Abuse is a Cycle

I know it may be hard to hear that you cannot help your abuser yourself. I know it might be even harder to hear that you need to put yourself first in this situation. There is no easy way out of abuse, and the reason it is so vital you remove yourself as soon as you can is because this is a cycle. The longer you stay and try to help, the more you get pulled into the cycle and the harder it becomes for you to leave.

The emotional abuse cycle comes in six parts. It starts with abuse, where your partner lashes out at you using humiliating or belittling behavior. They do this in order to maintain control and demonstrate that they are in charge.

Guilt comes after the abuse. Normally, your abuser will feel guilt over their actions. It is vital that I clarify that your abuser will generally feel guilt over potentially being caught, not because of the abuse they have subjected you to.

Excuses will follow their feelings of guilt. They will rationalize to you their behaviors, and even blame you for the reasons they abused you in the first place. They want to escape the responsibility of their actions.

For a brief moment, they will cycle through displays of normal behavior. In this phase, they will act as if nothing happened, they might even turn on extra charm to make the victim feel at ease. This lures the victim into a false sense of security.

After the phase of normal behavior passes, they enter into a fantasy period where they dream of regaining control over you again. Here they plan ways of punishing you for what they think you have done wrong.

Once the fantasy is over, they work to set up the scene where he can justify abusing you. After this, the abuse cycle starts over again. A victim can easily get re-trapped into this cycle once they find out their partner is emotionally abusing them. An abuser will make the victim feel like it is their fault and they deserve the treatment that they are receiving.

Breaking this cycle once you are aware of it will be important for your recovery and your psychological health. Emotional abuse is directly correlated with your psychological health; therefore, the more abuse you endure, the more work you will have to do to combat the feelings of depression, anxiety and PTSD.

Need More Answers?

Emotional abuse can be a tough situation to work out; I get it. It is understandable that you might be hesitant or concerned about your relationship. No-one wants to accuse their partner of emotional abuse, but no-one should want to put themselves in jeopardy either.

In a more direct black and white way, I have devised a list of signs you may be missing or ignoring in your relationship that can point to emotional abuse being present. They include:

- Being scared.

- Incessant lectures or painful comparisons to others from your partner.

- You are always at fault.

- They have possessive jealousy.

- They humiliate you and make big demands of you they know you cannot fulfill.

- They isolate you.

- They make you dependent on them.

- They think for you.

- When you think about how your relationship makes you feel, you mostly come up with negative emotions

These nine symptoms are a direct indication that you are being emotionally abused. If you feel like even one of these is an aspect of your relationship, talk to someone. It can even be someone you don't know, like a helpline. Sometimes saying it out loud to yourself can also make you realize the situation you are in.

Statistics on abuse are grim. According to the National Domestic Hotline, 24 people per minute are victims of some form of abuse. That is 24 people in sixty seconds! That means every 2.5 seconds there is a case of abuse being perpetrated against someone. That number leads to more than 12 million men and women being victims a year.

That number is staggering. These are the numbers for people who are in intimate relationships.

Why do they stay you ask. Well, it is the same reasons you might be questioning leaving your own relationship right now. People stay in abusive situations for a variety of reasons. Some of the most common involve fear. The fear of what will happen to them if they leave the relationship propels them to stay.

There are those that are used to abuse and believe that this type of behavior is normal. Those that find themselves in this situation might not know what a healthy relationship looks like, and since this is the behavior they are used to, they accept it.

A different dynamic in an LGBTQ (Lesbian, Gay, Bisexual, Questioning, and Transgender) relationship could be the fear of being outed. This means that they may not have come out to their friends or family yet, and their abuser could be threatening to out them if they left.

The effect of embarrassment and shame should not be underestimated in this situation. It is often hard or difficult for some people to face that they have been emotionally abused. This can stem from a fear of judgment from peers and family; they may even think they have done something wrong to end up in an abusive relationship and are embarrassed to say they made a mistake.

If you are in an emotionally abusive situation, you know the effect it can have on your self-esteem. Low self-esteem might be another reason a person stays in the cycle of abuse. When they are constantly put down by their partner, they might not believe that they deserve any better. They might think it is their fault that they are being treated this way. (If you feel this way, let me tell you, it is absolutely NOT your fault.)

—

Here comes the big one. Love. Many victims feel love for their abusive partner. This is not a weird thing to feel. It is expected that in an intimate romantic relationship there would be feelings of love attached. This emotion can be heightened if those involved have children. Their thoughts then would mainly be to keep their family together.

When love is involved, the victim often remembers how charming their partner was in the beginning. The victim might want the abusive behaviors to stop, but to keep the relationship going.

There are also cultural and religious reasons why people stay in abusive situations. Sometimes it seems like the better option to prevent bringing shame upon your family.

Immigration status can affect victims as well. If they are undocumented, they might worry that reporting or leaving the abusive situation could have an effect on their immigration status. Language barriers can be at play here too. It might be hard for a person whose first language is not the main language spoken in a country to communicate their experiences to those that can help.

A lack of money and resources can also compel a person to stay with an emotionally abusive partner. This can also fall under the umbrella of financial abuse; particularly if a victim is financially dependent on their partner.

When a person who is disabled feels physically dependent on their partner, it can cause a big issue for them to leave the safety they find in their abuser.

These are the main reasons people cannot leave their partners. Most of them cite a dependency on their partner, or a fear of being outed by their partners. This is never an easy situation to handle, and it can be even more complicated by children.

Keep in mind though that if you are suffering from emotional abuse, it does not mean your children are not. They could be just as harmed as you are.

Key Points

This last chapter covered a lot about emotional abuse. Before we move on, let us recap a few points:

- It is not your job to help your abuser.

- You are not at fault for your abuser's behavior. You do not deserve to feel worthless.

- Emotional abuse, like other abuse types, works in a cycle.

- The cycle goes from abuse to guilt, to excuses, normal behavior, fantasy, set-up, and right back to abuse again.

- It can be hard for a victim to break themselves away from a cycle of abuse.

- There are major signs to look out for that you might be suffering from emotional abuse.

- These signs can include being scared of your partner, put down by your partner and even cruelly compared to others by your partner.

- People tend to stay in abusive relationships for an assortment of reasons. It is important to understand these and be conscious of them if you are trying to help a loved one out of an abusive situation.

In the next few chapters, we will explore safety planning and a roadmap to your way out of an abusive situation.

Section 3: Talking About Emotional Abuse

Chapter Seven: Talking it out

So, You Want to Work it out

It is natural to want to work things out with someone that you have dedicated time and energy to. For those who were initially unaware of the ways in which an emotional abuser treats their victims, by this point in the book you should have a clearer idea. You should now be equipped with the tools to differentiate the line between being human and being abusive.

Some of you might still want to work things out with your partner, despite their abusive behavior. Maybe they have not hit extremes yet, and you think there is still a way to save the relationship. Whatever your reasons are, they are valid. As long as you ensure that you get the help, you need to process how the cycle of emotional abuse has affected you.

So, what do you do when you want to work on things? How do you approach discussing emotional abuse with your partner in a healthy way? What happens if you get stuck in the cycle when they blame you again?

Excellent questions! Well, in this next section we discuss exactly how to approach these questions with your partner.

You might also be wondering if it is worth trying to save your relationship or talk it out with your partner. You might not know the answer to this initially. That is okay. I suggest talking with a professional. Get in touch with a therapist and talk to them about your feelings and concerns. They can help you work through your feelings about the relationship.

If you choose to talk to your partner on your own, do so in a way that is going to make them feel loved and supported. Remember that if you are dealing with someone that absolutely cannot have a conversation about the relationship without it blowing up into a fight, this person is never going to have the ability to communicate in a healthy way and therefore the relationship is doomed unless you both commit to seeing a professional therapist.

If this is not the case and you feel safe enough to have a one on one conversation, do so in a way that is helpful, not critical. Your partner does not need to hear that they are an abuser or that they are manipulative etc. No one wants to hear those negative things about themselves. Instead, keep the conversation focused on you.

Tell them that you've been feeling a little overwhelmed or upset by the relationship lately. Try to phrase things in a way that completely removes the word "you" from the conversation. For example: "You always disregard my feelings" turns into "when I hear my feelings disregarded, it makes me feel really upset". "You never let me go out" turns into "I would like to have some more time to go out and see my friends. That would make me feel really happy."

If you make your partner the enemy, they will never be on your side. An abuser likely struggles with communication, so you are going to have to practice healthier communication to pick up the slack of your partner.

Another option is to take some time out. Take a vacation with the girls or the guys, even if it's just for a weekend getaway or camping trip. Try to find a way to spend multiple days without your partner so that you can see things in a clearer light. This will also help you analyze your feelings. Does being away from your partner help you feel more relaxed? Does the thought of going back home to them make you feel anxious? Pay attention to what feelings are being caused after you have certain thoughts.

In a healthy and normal relationship, you should genuinely feel excitement to see your partner after some time away. You should miss them and want to spend more time with them.

During your time away, you might be able to make clear choices if you do not feel like you are tied to them or owe them an answer. If it is impossible for you to get some alone time because your partner does not let you, this is emotional abuse and you are in a very unhealthy relationship.

While emotional abuse is an extremely distressing form of abuse for the human psyche, there are still levels to how badly the abuser is perpetrating these behaviors. Keep in mind that what works for you might not work for someone else. As humans, we all operate and think differently, so not every solution fits the situation. That is why open communication with your partner and being honest with yourself is so important.

The Occasional Abuser

Let me get this out of the way right now. If you did the quizzes and have read the book up until this point, and you still find yourself justifying your partner's abusive behavior, STOP. Abuse is abuse. An occasional abuser is still an abuser. Remember I said earlier that abuse is not an opinion. You do not get to draw that line on your own.

Bear in mind I am not talking about your partner having a bad human moment and yelling too loud, or saying something they probably regret later. I am talking about emotionally abusive behavior that has been described in the course of this book, where you experience emotions such as fear, feelings of isolation and even start to question your own self-worth due to your partner's emotional abuse.

If your partner emotionally abuses you, but it happens only occasionally, be aware that this is a misconception. Your partner's abuse cycle takes longer to cycle back to where you can feel the abuse happening to you. It does not mean that they are not abusing you and that you are okay.

Any amount of emotional abuse can cause feelings of depression and anxiety, so it is essential that you understand that your case and your feelings are still very real and very important, even if you only feel like the abuse occurs on an occasional basis.

If you want to work things out in a situation where you feel like you are being occasionally abused, that is okay too; you need to understand what to expect going into a conversation with someone who might be defensive about their behaviors. Prepare yourself for the probability that your partner might blame you as well for their abusive behavior. Read ahead to find some clues and tips on how to have such a sensitive conversation.

The Talk Environment

Using the right phrasing for the talk is important but doing it in a healthy environment will also contribute to a healthy conversation. Talking to someone about their abusive behavior is never an easy task, especially if the person is adept at masking or concealing their behaviors.

Something you might find comfort from doing is to get a journal and write things down. Write down the ways in which they emotionally abuse you and how it affects you. If you think that your partner might be gaslighting you, a journal will be particularly helpful so that you can keep track of what was said and what was done in situations that your partner tries to twist.

Another option in addition to the journal or beside it can be to have a neutral third party sit in on your conversation to be a mediator and support. This person should not incite an argument or fight, but know how to diffuse the situation. This person is normally called an emotional shield as they act as a buffer between you and your emotional abuser.

These confrontations might not be occurring between a romantic partnership. It could be a parent, a child, a sibling, and even a friend that you share a relationship with. Emotional abuse is not strictly reserved for intimate relationships and can happen in any relationship where two people are active participants in.

While it may seem unconventional to most, another way to put a shield between you and your abuser is to conduct the conversation over the telephone. You always risk that they might end the call without completely hearing you out, but if there is not a third party you trust to act as an emotional shield, this is another solution.

Conducting such a sensitive conversation where you confront your abuser about their behavior over the phone can be challenging, but it provides a safe space where they have to hear you out, and it makes it harder for them to emotionally manipulate you back into their cycle of abuse.

If you do have a person that you trust and use as an emotional shield during this very difficult conversation, consider having it in a public area. You can try a semi-public area where you can still have some privacy, but the person you are confronting is forced to keep their voice down and listen to what you have to say.

It is actually important that, as a victim, you decide where and how to confront your abuser if you choose to do so. The reason for this is because this is your first step in reclaiming your power in decision-making. This will be your first attempt at controlling an area and situation in your life.

If you have a friend that you are concerned about, approach the subject with them carefully. Be aware that they might not be receptive to your thoughts about their relationship. Respect what decision they make, and aim to be their support. They might realize it on their own and, when they do, they will need you in their corner.

The most crucial part you can play is to be their support system when they realize what kind of situation they are in. By being there for them, you can ensure that their feelings of isolation are lessened, and it is more likely that they will come to you for help. Be patient and be there. Those are the two best things you can do as a friend to someone in an emotionally abusive situation.

Dealing with Your Realization

So, now you are at the point where you may have just realized that you are in an abusive situation. Maybe it has just dawned on you, or perhaps you have fully accepted the fact that your relationship is an unhealthy one.

That is a good start, and I know it's not easy. The first step in solving any problem is identifying that there is one in the first place. If you can identify that you are being emotionally abused, you have taken solid steps towards fixing the problem. Remember that you are in control of your own life. You don't need to listen or bow down to anyone's expectations or demands of you. Also keep in mind that there are levels of emotional abuse. Some abusers can penetrate deep into a victim's psyche and cause high levels of harm; while other abusive situations are milder and do not cross as many lines. Regardless of the level of abuse, emotional abuse should still be taken seriously but, the level of abuse you might experience from your partner can severely impact your willingness to continue or end the relationship.

Whether you choose to stay in the relationship, work on

the relationship or walk away, is completely up to you. Some people decide that they have nothing more to say and they want to find their way out of the relationship and towards themselves again. Other people that decide to leave might still want to confront their abuser.

Once you deal with your realization, it really depends on you what your next step is. For those that want to leave immediately, chapter eight will have some great tips on creating a safety plan!

If you decide you want to confront your abuser, keep reading for some more tips and clues. Talking to them might make you feel better, or you might have hopes of working things out. That's great. If, for some reason you find that even after talking it out you are unable to continue a relationship with the person, then chapter eight will have some great information for you as well.

Steps to Confronting Your Abuser

The first step mentioned above is to see and recognize the cycle of abuse you are in. After this is done, it can be cathartic to speak it out loud. Try and identify all the tactics of abuse that are being used against you, and then say them out loud. Say them out loud so many times that it becomes second nature, almost like saying them is equivalent to you taking a breath. Take control of the words until you are sure your abuser cannot take them from you and manipulate them.

It is important to do this BEFORE confronting your abuser. It will give you the necessary courage and certainty needed to ensure you do not waiver in the conversation. Remember when you are confronting your abuser the goal is not to argue or yell at them. You want to approach them quietly. This way they know you are serious, and the less hysterical you are in the conversation, the less chance they have to manipulate and turn the situation around.

When you confront your abuser, and you are able to speak to them calmly, give them a chance to realize what you are saying. They might need time to process that their own behaviors are abusive. Remember, many abusers do not know what they are doing is emotionally abusive.

If, during your conversation, they still do not back down or admit to their behaviors, use phrases that highlight their behavior as abusive. Stand your ground. This part of the conversation is where an emotional shield might also be helpful.

Some key phrases you might use with someone who is being emotionally abusive are:

- Your stare is not going to intimidate me.

- It is not okay for you to belittle me/call me by that name.

- That story does not embarrass me.

- I will not be coerced into doing something I do not want to do.

The goal of your conversation with your abuser is to come to a resolution, not to start an argument, so be firm but gentle when you are talking to them. Even if you decide to end the relationship, remain steadfast in your reasons why and do not incite an argument where they can manipulate you.

If you have confronted your abuser and have decided to stay together but you notice that the abusive behavior is continuing, it is time to stress your boundaries. Talk to them again and be very clear about what your boundaries are and where they lie.

Stressing the seriousness of your talk with the abuser can be to instill consequences for breaking boundaries. Let them know that you will not tolerate the behavior anymore. For emotionally abusive situations, an example can be when an abuser forces you to try and do something by making you feel guilty. Be clear with them that you will not do things out of guilt, and they cannot coerce you. Let them know as well that the consequence is that you will not conform to what they want out of fear.

Being clear about your boundaries is one of the best things you can do when you are in an emotionally abusive situation you are trying to fix, but sometimes your words can seem empty.

The hardest part about confronting your abuser can be to stand by your decisions and boundaries. Once you have laid a boundary down for your abuser, it is crucial that you stand firmly by your decision. Let them know what the consequences are, and then carry out the consequences if they continue the abusive behavior.

Do not let yourself fall back into the cycle of abuse. This is where having someone hold you accountable as the victim can be helpful. Let a third party who is aware of your situation know what your boundaries are. When they hold you accountable, you are more likely to feel stronger in your decisions, and it will be easier to stand by your decisions with support, even if one of those decisions is walking away from your abuser.

Key Points

A lot of information regarding standing up to and talking to your abuser was covered in this chapter. It is never an easy task to sit face-to-face with someone who has messed with your head – whether they are doing it unwittingly or not. The repercussions of being the victim of emotional abuse can be long-lasting. Let's go over a few key elements about talking to an abuser:

- Wanting to work things out with your abuser is okay.

- An abuser can be an intimate partner, a parent, sibling, friend or even an employer.

- Sometimes you need an emotional shield with

you when you are talking to an abuser.

- If you do not want another person present, you can conduct the conversation through the phone.

- Choosing where and when the meeting takes place is crucial to regaining back some control that has been taken from you. It is also important to demonstrate to your abuser that you are not going to be manipulated anymore.

- Practice saying how they are abusing you out loud.

- Do not go into the conversation expecting a fight. Try and be calm about the situation. Be gentle when speaking to them, but firm.

- Let them know there are consequences to their abusive behavior.

- Stand by your consequences and decisions.

- Having someone hold you accountable as the victim can ensure you do not fall back into an emotionally abusive cycle.

Sometimes you can work things out with your abuser. Therapy can make a big difference in both yours and the abuser's lives. Many relationships in which emotional abuse played a role can be salvaged and worked on. It is not uncommon, and you are definitely not in the wrong if you want to work things out.

But there is a line where people cross into the territory of being too emotionally abusive. In these situations, you will want to find your way out. Maybe you have tried to make it work, or maybe you are just once and for all done, and you want to walk away from the situation. That is okay too. In the next chapter, we will go over how you can safely leave the situation you are in.

Section 4: A Roadmap Out

Chapter Eight: It is Time to Leave

You Have Decided to Leave

This is the moment. You have decided that the relationship is over and that it is time to leave. Either your partner had crossed too many lines into abusive territory, or they did not respect your boundaries when you confronted them about their abusive behaviors.

You might remember when I mentioned the fact that when a victim is leaving their abuser, that is the most dangerous time for them. This fact still remains true; however, do not be scared. This is why you picked this book up, for support and guidance. That is exactly what I am about to give you.

Firstly, know that what you are doing is not an easy

decision. It takes time, pain and loss to get to the stage that you are at. Removing yourself from your emotional abuser's web can be tricky and difficult. If children are involved, it can make the situation more complicated, but it can still be done.

Secondly, know that your safety, emotionally and physically, should be your priority. My goal for this chapter is to give you a guideway to getting yourself safely out of an abusive situation. I know it can be concerning, but you have made it this far.

You have been on quite the journey. You learned about some common misconceptions when it comes to emotional abuse. You have also learned what signs to look out for in your relationships if you are being emotionally abused. If you are the friend of someone you are concerned about, then you have learned that the best thing you can do is be there for them. Do not cut them out of your life because they cannot leave their situation on your schedule.

Maybe you learned that you are the abuser. Hopefully, once you learned that information you took advantage of my suggestions and spoke to a therapist regarding your issues. You also need to be upfront and honest with your partner about what you have been doing. Remember, it does not have to be the end of the relationship, but you do have to put in the work to learn how to modify your abusive behavior.

Leaving with Children

For those that have children with their abuser, it is especially complicated and emotional. It can be a tough choice to decide to remove your children with you. Keep in mind though that children are not immune to emotional abuse. If the abuser is not abusing them too, they can see and feel the effects emotional abuse has on you.

Some emotional abusers threaten to take your kids away from you if you leave. If you are in a relationship with an abuser who has crossed many boundaries, then you might have already heard their threats. There are lots of tactics that abusers use in order to put your children in between the two of you. These tactics may include trying to turn the children against you, emotionally abusing the children, taking the children and not returning them to you, and even calling immigration, depending on your status, to have the state remove your children from your care.

I know you might be freaking out, but you need to know what to expect and look for when planning to leave your abuser. Relax. Breathe. You need to devise a safety plan.

Safety planning is crucial when you are trying to leave an abuser. A safety plan is a plan of action you come up with – sometimes with help – that can help you map out how to handle dangerous situations and how to react to abusive situations.

Remind your children that their job is to stay safe and not to protect you. Have a place where they can safely meet up, and a code word that lets them know when it is safe to leave their meet-up place. Direct your children where and how to get help if it is not safe.

Pack a bag with emergency items for you and your children. Include all their important documents. If you do not have a safe place to store it, leave the bag with a friend or someone you trust. Remember that there are family advocates and shelters that can help you and give you advice. If you do not know about the resources in your town, go to the National Domestic Violence website, and you can chat with someone who will help you out.

Memorize numbers and have your children do it too if they can, just in case you get left without a phone. Understand that if you do leave with your abuser's children, custody is an issue. It is vital you speak to a lawyer, and you know your options. You do not want to break any laws or have to keep running once you get away from your abuser.

Creating A Safety Plan

For anyone in an abusive situation, it is important to create a safety plan. It can be one you write down, or even one that you memorize and keep in your head. There are a few vital steps I will walk you through to help you with your safety plan.

If you are being emotionally abused, keep any evidence you can, as emails and messages are your best friend in this situation. If they threaten you, save the messages. Take pictures of them if you have to.

Tell someone what is happening to you. It does not have to be a friend or family member. Reach out to someone who is a professional dealing with abusive situations if you have to. Telling someone ensures that you are not the only person that knows about your situation.

If you can, try setting money aside. With an abuser that controls your finances, this can be hard. Ask your family or friends if you can, to keep money aside for you.

When leaving, make sure that you have some important information such as your identification on you. Any legal documents might be a good idea to have a copy with as well – marriage license or deed to a home if you share a home with your abuser. These can also include medical records or work permits.

Once you leave an abusive situation, change your routine. Switch work schedules, and change your phone number. Do not stay in the same routine your abuser was accustomed to. Consider renting a post office box for your mail so that your abuser cannot track you down that way. If you have a restraining order, keep a copy of it on you.

It is vital that once you remove yourself from the

situation, you surround yourself with people who are emotionally supportive. Set achievable goals for yourself and then work towards them. Focus on your recovery.

Treat yourself kindly. When you are coming from an emotionally abusive situation, it can be easy to forget that you need to be kind and gentle with yourself as well. Give yourself time to heal and remember that you are worthy.

If you are a friend or loved one, your best safety plan is to be supportive. Listen to them, and help connect them to resources. Do not share their location or other private information with anyone else or on social media. Helping a victim whom you love can be frustrating when they do not do what you think they should. Be patient; everyone processes abuse in his or her own ways.

Key Points

This chapter was mainly about finding a way out for yourself. Some of the most important tips to remember are to:

- Make a safety plan.

- A safety plan can be for you and your children, or just you.

- Try your best not to leave important documents behind.

- Change your routine. Change places you shop and visit.

- Lean on friends and family.

- Give yourself time to heal.

- Be kind to yourself.

I will say it one more time; because to someone who has been emotionally abused, this is the most important information you will hear: Be kind to yourself.

GET YOUR
FREE
10 DAY SELF CARE CHALLENGE

—

*10 Days of Actionable Tasks
all in one PDF*

VISIT:
*millennialships.com/free-
self-care-challenge*

Conclusion

There are no words to express how a person feels in a situation where abuse is involved but, as a victim, you cannot give up on yourself.

By now, you have read through the book, done the quiz, and hopefully you have learned some valuable information about emotional abuse and how to get yourself out if you find yourself in this situation.

Emotional abuse is considered domestic violence. Just because you do not have a physical bruise on your body, does not make your case any less serious.

Reach out to those that can help you. If you struggle finding someone to trust, call the National Domestic Violence Hotline at 1-800-799-SAFE (7233), or 1-800-787-3224. They will be able to provide you with resources. If you do not want to call, you can also chat with a representative on your phone. They have amazing resources for victims that might be deaf or hard-of-hearing as well.

Their website www.thehotline.org also has

information and resources that can help someone who is in an abusive situation.

I have also created an online hub for women to read about scientific ways to help with self care, anxiety and relationships. If you are interested in viewing my blog content you can check it out at Millennialships.com.

Remember to think about yourself first and stay safe.

References

Abuse Defined | The National Domestic Violence Hotline. (2018). Retrieved from https://www.thehotline.org/is-this-abuse/abuse-defined/

Abuse Types and Cycle Wheel. (2013). Retrieved from http://www.ashleighspatienceproject.com/abuse-types-and-cycle-wheel.html

Desanctis, E. (2018). What Emotional Abuse Really Means. Retrieved from https://www.joinonelove.org/learn/emotional-abuse-really-means/

Hammond, C. (2018). How to Confront an Abusive Person. Retrieved from https://pro.psychcentral.com/exhausted-woman/2016/05/how-to-confront-an-abusive-person/

Law, J. (2017). Are you being emotionally abused? Take this quiz to find out. Retrieved from https://interact.support/are-you-being-emotionally-abused/

Mathews, A. (2016). When Is It Emotional Abuse?. Retrieved from https://www.psychologytoday.com/us/blog/traversing-the-inner-terrain/201609/when-is-it-emotional-abuse

Patricelli, K. (2018). Types of Abuse. Retrieved from

https://www.mentalhelp.net/articles/types-of-abuse/

Safety Planning | Loveisrespect.org. (2018). Retrieved from https://www.loveisrespect.org/for-yourself/safety-planning/

What is Gaslighting? | The National Domestic Violence Hotline. (2014). Retrieved from https://www.thehotline.org/2014/05/29/what-is-gaslighting/